Let's talk about...

NATALYA AKINSHINA

LET'S TALK ABOUT...

iUniverse books may be ordered through booksellers or by contacting:

iUniverse
1663 Liberty Drive
Bloomington, IN 47403
www.iuniverse.com
844-349-9409

Because of the dynamic nature of the Internet, any web addresses or links contained in this book may have changed since publication and may no longer be valid. The views expressed in this work are solely those of the author and do not necessarily reflect the views of the publisher, and the publisher hereby disclaims any responsibility for them.

Any people depicted in stock imagery provided by Getty Images are models, and such images are being used for illustrative purposes only. Certain stock imagery © Getty Images.

ISBN: 978-1-6632-5162-6 (sc)
ISBN: 978-1-6632-5163-3 (e)

Library of Congress Control Number: 2023904690

Print information available on the last page.

iUniverse rev. date: 03/13/2023

You

You are like a water flow
born from dazzling ice
and fluffy coldest snow;
next to blue shining sky...
And you are like a water... rushing
into the boundless ocean,
filled with wind and freedom,
magical wild emotion...
My lovely gift from heaven,
You may be cold or hot,
Turn into prickly snowflakes
Or gentle weightless fog.
You are my lovely water
You bring me back again
I love you, no matter,
My gentle summer rain.
And every time you come back
As tender water drops.
I feel I love you... love you,
And I cannot it stop!
There's no need to be sad
and suffer on your own,
I'll wait for your decision,
No matter how long...

Taking chances

My life is not a straight way,
It's lace, made by myself,
It gets sophisticated…
Not simpler with new days.
My life is lace-like twisting,
It's an ups-and-down train.
I lose or find something
or someone day by day.
Does time is a tool of healing?
Seriously? Who said that?
Can time delete my feelings?
Sad memories? Regrets?
But I'm not a cold stone…
not any more to say…
My fragile heart is not to blame,
It wants to find the same…
I know that you love me
and ready taking chance…
My soul flies to love again
like a butterfly to fire.
Agreed… It is not easy,
I think it takes a while…
But sure, I need a loving
and open heart nearby.

Finding My Kind Wizard

I wanna find a kind wizard
To turn me into a fairy breeze...
I wanna fly to you through seas,
To hug you... banish any blizzards.
I wanna find a kind wizard
To make me into gentle rain...
I wanna wipe away your tears,
To be with you through joy and pain.
I wanna find a kind wizard,
To light up more blue shining sky.
I wanna gently warm your winter season,
To always make your eyes shine bright.
I wanna find a kind wizard
To turn me into a blossom field.
I wanna charm with nature wisdom,
To save you with this lovely shield.
My darling, trust me please,
Hug me and give me only a kiss.
I'll be your private wizard, especially for you,
I can be anything you want because I deeply love you.

Whisper of My Heart

What's life? It's just a moment as a flash.
Like all of us, I'm a vortex splash.
A world of atoms meets for a while
To give us be... and feel alive.
You are a light vortex, I'm alike.
Like a breeze, not flurry, blast, or storm.
I'm not the type to hurt or strike...
I am for a hug, caress, and warm.
We are all made of the selfsame atoms,
With own face and own thoughts.
There are so many different characters,
Like music... with only seven notes.
I am the wind, my life is pace,
I feel it's wrong we're apart.
While every day you're embraced...
It's me, hear the whisper of my heart.
We are here for a while.
Try to do everything on time.
If you don't have some plans for me.
I will disappear... totally...
I am the wind, I do not shout,
I don't make noise... I don't pursue.
Can't you feel me? I can't cry out,
As wind, I whisper "I love you"...

Dreams

Wave after wave, perpetual motion...
The water washes all traces into the ocean.
And all things repeat, day after day...
Life brings us something, or takes away...
I'm losing myself, when my cheek touches yours.
I'm sinking... I surrender to you without any wars...
Looking into your eyes and flying away,
I'm ready to cry... that's a wonderful day!
I hold you in my arms, hug and caress you.
I lost my heart in your eyes and feel only deep tenderness.
There is nothing to say... no things I can't do...
I just whisper and whisper how much I love you...
Wind, water, rocks, and salt spray...
Delight! I'm crazy, I call you by name...
You're the light of my life, I want to tell so much...
I promise to be there for you; and saying
how deeply I'm touched...
We are embracing... You're smiling at me...
I'm burning like fire... so happy and free.

A new spring

When you look at me,
I just want to smile.
You don't say anything...
Maybe wait for a while?...
While my hope was gone...
My heart beats stronger...
A new spring has come!
I feel your love... I can't wait longer...
I thought my heart had calmed down;
and nothing new was expected...
When I saw your eyes, I was trapped;
a new love was selected.
I thought that all has been behind,
But feel that flowers decided
To bloom not only in my garden,
but also in my heart... inside me.
Should I sing a new song?
This is unusual and strange.
I'm used to being alone...
I'm afraid of any changes.

Living for the Little Things

Someone wisely told me:
"Live for the little things…"
for each dawn and sunset,
for raindrops in the springs.
Live for the singing of birds;
for adventures, travels and meetings…
Live for seeing blue sky and white clouds…
Savor these moments… they are so fleeting.
Live for the dance
For laughter to pain.
Live for your music… romance…
Warm conversations in the cold rain…
Live for light smiles…
for happiness in loved eyes.
Live for sweet whisper to lover
in the mornings and nights.
Live for the sake of people
who remember what you drink…
coffee without?… or with sugar?…
or you prefer as longer to sleep…
I am trying to come by this not easy way…
Do you hear brave and reckless my heart?
It rejoices and sings … so glad that it can …
can decide instead of me… and command.

Mirage

Look at me, don't ask me why.
I follow your gentle gaze,
No matter where, no matter why.
Agreed, it is a crazy case.
I want to say "you're a mirage",
You are somewhere far away,
White sun on endless pale blue sky,
Black, red or yellow day.
Hot, empty, flat infinity,
All melted from the heat,
And nothing else on lonely way,
No chance to meet or greet.
No matter how, no matter why,
In the hot and swaying air,
I see green trees and clear sky,
A cool lake with fresh water there.
Why do I trust you so much?
You didn't send me any signs,
I can't see anything around,
Just lovely eyes, your brown eyes.
One more step towards you,
And one more breath, more sigh,
So windy, sandy, dusty,
With a hot gray, dirty sky.

No strength, trust ends, and only
Hot flame remains inside,
More steps... I'm so lonely,
You are still not in sight.
I'm looking for... still waiting...
But no blue, no green...

And only sand and air dust...
Grey, red, and yellow wind.
I really want... I want to trust!
Don't let me get away!
I really love you... love you... just...
Just show me my way!

The Melody of Love

I wanna sing to you, my love,
Like crazy nightingale in May.
Forget all fears, you are beloved,
I wanna heal your heart this way.
I feel myself a brave and saucy,
Just look at me. Believe…
I'll do my best, my lovely bossy,
and give you everything you need.
I'll always stand by you
No matter what…
It's only time for me and you.
I'll try to give you all you want...
Trust me... as I believe in you.
Just trust me, honey… don't give up...
I live by you, admire you...
Just look! ...The Sun is rising up!
All birds are singing and rejoicing.
It's time! Wake up, my love, wake up…
Let's dream together, darling,
I am in love with you...
Addicted like a child and mad because of you...
I'm calling you. Forget control...
This is the melody of love.
Just hear me, open your soul…
Feel touch... My lovely gentle dove!

Thoughts out loud

Can tell me why?... Why music of your soul
did not respond to whisper of my heart...
I'll try again.... and one more roll...
My heart cannot agree to be apart.
It seemed to me again... my darling heart of glass...
Isn't that you? Another crazy day...
When will you come to me at last?
I wait for you and see you everywhere...
I'm happy getting words from you!
Again... my mind doesn't know frames!
But stop! It's not for me ... it's not from you...
I would be crazy through your game!...
As crazy child... I'm talking to your songs...
And everywhere I see some special words...
Agree with me! Something is wrong...
Take back my mind, my lovely ghost...
Such kind of love... type of communications...
It's not for me... It kills my aspirations...
Agree... huge ocean is between us...
A lot of years... and red dividing lines...
You changed my life and I feel free...
I can burn out in this flame.
Please, talk to me... just talk to me.
My life will never be the same...

Hugs

I miss you very much…
I want you to be here.
I want to talk to you,
and listen to your voice,
look to your lovely eyes,
I wanna kiss and hug you…
But you are not around.
What should I really do?
They say that any person
needs eight-ten hugs in a day.
It's need for our good health!
It's seriously! no play.
That's why, I hugged all colleagues,
my relatives and friends,
all girls and boys I met…
(one, two, three, four… and ten)
I hugged my dogs and hugged my cats
(plus one, two, three, four, five, six …eight)
I chased chinchillas for half day…
and hugged all furry ones again:
one - Chaplin, triple - Hickey, Milky - twice…
I still feel so lonely…
I don't need any wise advice!
I want to hug YOU only!

Twenty-three hours

Twenty-three hours are between me and you.
Only twenty-three hours... and I could be with you.
It's a lifetime... but less than one day...
I'm flying to you. It is my choice and my way...
One gentle touch... My mind flies away...
Look into my eyes. Is that all we may?
Only twenty-three hours... Let me step to you.
May we have a talk? Don't let me leave you.
Flame is burning inside, it's my love, it's my light.
My soul flies away like a star rain in the night.
it goes out in infinity dark. I can't wait anymore...
no one little spark. No more... no more...
Do you want me to tell you about you?
Well, listen to me. How do I imagine you?
So, you're very strong... But fragile and soft.
You are very smart, with rational mind,
You are emotional with open light heart.
Your voice sounds powerful... loud...
but you love to hear silence and heart's beat...
You are surrounded by a crowd...
but you need only one... really need...
You live in a city... huge, noisy and gray...
but you love solitude and prefer sounds of rain,
you like rustling of leaves in warm windy day...
you are waiting white snow like a baby again...
Twenty-three hours are between me and you.
Only twenty-three hours... and I could be with you...

Silence in response

It's raining. What a heavy rain!
My eyes are closed. I cry alone.
I told I love you. .. How could I may?
It's better to be hid; it's safe to be unknown.
Why did I tell you this?
Drops trickle down all my face,
And wash away all salty tears.
I've broken all in any case.
How stupid and painfully hopeless!
You didn't hear any words.
I feel me broken and defenseless.
And only silence... in response...
You're used to hear such kind of words.
They don't mean anything to you...
They fly away my heart like birds...
Why does my heart so yearn for you?
You don't need tenderness... my lips..
Why does it hurt me so much?
I closed my eyes... can't stop my tears.
You didn't say and didn't touch...
It's rain... Rainwater sweeps away all tears,
but can't clean up this pain...
I can't do anything, my sweet...
No speak... no laughing ... only rain...
I feel the rainbow inside is turning gray...
All color stripes become so pale...
Why does my heart so yearn for you?
You are reward and biggest pain.
What's that?... I feel something... and open eyes...
Through the water and tears I'm seeing you...
"Don't feel sorry for me... It is nice...

No, it's just raining... no any tears... I'm fine with you..."
You're taking my hands... You're just as wet through...
I see tears in your eyes... "I'm sorry! Are you in pain?"
I whisper that love you... You say me the same...
What's that? Do you feel the same way?!
Were you waiting for me for a long?!...
Oh my Got!!! Let the world now is waiting for us...
I can hear your heart beating so faster and strong.
I kiss you... and feel... *j'ai beaucoup de tendresse*....

One dream tonight

Don't love me, my love!
Don't hug me my funny.
Don't kiss me, my sweet.
Don't miss me, my honey!
Loving is painful. Suffering is deadly.
Longing is tiring. Crying is badly.
Why do you need fondness?
Why do you need affection?
Why do you need tenderness?
and some gentle reflections?
You don't need feelings.
You don't need emotions.
Enough impressions already!
No need any motions!
Do not trust anyone. There are no fairy tales.
Dream no more! You don't need scarlet sails.
...I woke up at once!
What a terrible dream!
Oh my God! You're next to me...
I don't want such kind of extreme!...
Love me, my love!
Hug me my funny.
Kiss me, my sweet.
Miss me, my honey!

My stupid heart

Someone sometimes can't hear
not even voice or shout.
The other hears your thoughts,
and whisper of your heart.
I didn't know before
that heart can bitterly cry.
Why I've been waiting for...
You told me nothing... Why?
Don't cry my stupid heart.
I understand you well.
You don't want be apart
You need to be with *belle*.
I didn't know before
that love can hurt so much.
I don't want feel it more.
But I am really touched...
You did me nothing, honey,
No actions, no words...
Stop silence... say me something
Because it really hurts.
My heart in love is crying...
I'm really hurt and lonely...
I'm going crazy, darling.
I'm calling you, you only.
I wanna feel your heartbeat.
I love and miss you. Why?
Is this my life? Such is my fate?
My stupid heart, don't cry!
I'm going crazy, dearest,
because of only you.
I'd like to dream and talk with you.

Say me you need me too.
I wanna kiss you. Give me hug…
and try to listen to my heart.
Let's try to talk about love,
Stop being silent, my sweetheart.

Magic drugs for soul

The soul comes into this world
To learn to love... with love to be.
Your life began with love. Thanks Lord!
We're here learning love... Believe...
Don't try to go back to past.
Life goes on. It wasn't last...
Was it so terrible or pleasant?
It always kills the present... Trust...
Love stories don't repeat themselves.
Don't wait for anyone from past.
Go ahead! Who really needs you,
Catch up with you. Intrust... Just trust...!
We think that don't have time today...
tomorrow we won't have any strength...
We won't be here on one day...
Do not delay and live today!
I want to be your medicine...
Your magic drugs for soul.
We don't need no vaccine,
Injections... Special goal!
The soul can be healed
By Humor, Love and Nature.
Then we could add some Music,
Some Dancing and Adventure...
Let's try to test it... do it!
Are you afraid? Come on!
My lovely friend, my honey,
Canadian Dion!

My gifts for you

I left my home to be alone,
To try to heal my heart and soul.
I talk to rivers, winds and stones...
I wander all day long alone...
It doesn't matter where I go...
I think about only you.
It doesn't matter what I do...
I say your name and dream of you.
I want to give you blue-blue sky!
Its wind and endless white-blue space!
There are no boundaries! Just fly!
Feel free and choose your lovely place!
I want to give you star named Sun!
This godly fire grants us warmth!
Its the eternal light of life.
Take all sunsets, sunrises, rainbows...
I want to give you my Tien-Shan!
Its pure majesty and brilliance.
That helps to see essence of life.
Let's take its power and learn resilience.
I wanna give you a fairy tale.
It's so kind and funny.
There's bound to be a happy end.
I want to make you joyful, honey.
I wanna give you all relish...
Feel crazy flavor of wild herbs!
Blue thyme and purple sage
enfold my hair, my face and hands...
It's not so sweet and no embellish
like Scotish heather's blue-blue fields...

It's not so sharp and no swelish
as French lavender purple seas...
This fragrance is continual,
Soft, tender, so deep...
This crazy smell like love to you.
I hope one day you'll feel it.

My apologies

Forgive me, please,
That I've been late a little.
Forgive me all your sorrows and tears.
You know life is so fragile... so brittle...
Forgive me, please... forgive me, please, for this...
Forgive me, please,
Your lonely nights and all your fears.
I didn't hug you... didn't kiss...
I will not leave you anymore.
I haven't been with you for years...
Believe me... and forgive me, please.
Forgive me, please,
for all unspoken tender words,
For all sunsets... sunrises spent alone.
For Christmas holidays
without me, my fairy bird...
Life's passing, so fleeting... don't postpone...
Forgive me, please,
I'm not so young, and not the prettiest;
I'm not so shining, cheerful, wise and bliss...
Not so lucky, not the strongest... not the richest...
Forgive me, please... forgive me all of this.
Forgive me, please...
Just take my hand and let me stand by you.
My eyes sparkle like emeralds
when I just think about you.
They'll tell you everything...
We don't need any words.
Just look at me...
Believe me, my lovely firebird.
Don't count any wrinkles.

Instead... Look into my eyes.
They'll never lie to you.
Just tell me that you need me...
Believe and recognize...
My eyes – the best of mirrors…
They love you so much!
Forgive me, please...
My soul is drawn to you,
We've never met... and never touched...
I want to go mad with gentle loving you.
Forgive me for not being...
not being me the best...
Kiss me... I want to go crazy
with awesome happiness.

To my son

Everything's been going in another way today....
It's summer outside... it's very raining day.
You know well how much I love this big drop rain.
But this is so unusual... Son's birthday day today...
The Sun is shining brightly... surprising summer rain...
Cool summer rain... It's all the other way...
My mind is getting crazy by reason of this rain...
I feel my age today... you know why...
So many years have passed... Days fly...
The same cool rain was in the hottest summer time.
Thank you, for choosing me your mom...
I dreamed tonight your little palm...
It was a miracle. You chose me... Right?
My little angel...you're always my life light.
You've been a man for a long time...
I'm still your angel guardian...
Some things are always in my mind...
I am foolhardy in...
I always died from endless tenderness...
Your smiles and cry... your kisses, hugs...
I still remember everything... And sleepless nights...
The joy and happiness from your first steps,
Your looks and smiles...
The first your words ... your endless questions...
Your crazy love to dogs and cats...
Your first small fish... your bicycles...
Your lovely skateboard, chess, spikenards...
I still remember everything..
and your first love... and your love wounds.
Margot… and Julia… and Ellen...
My heart was torn by the same pain...

You looks like me... you're a romantic;
And need someone to love.
Be healthy, happy, lucky, loved!
I look at you... from down to up,
you will be always in my heart...
You are my flesh... you are my blood.
You are my man, the most beloved.
I love so many things like you...
I love the rain,... "be free and independent"...
I read all books to you before...
right now take some after you, the ones you recommended...
Raindrops flow down slowly on tear-stained glass...
I'd like the traces in my soul can disappear so fast...
Time is like a huge black hole
collecting all your past…
It really takes our everything,
but returns nothing us...
I want to love and be in love.
I want the same you want!
You're so young... you're so strong...
But, I am really not ...
My heart is asking for last Love.
Hey, don't be jealous, darling.
You are always in my heart...
You are always in my mind....

Letter «C»

There is evening... and nothing to do...
So... I'm looking the Oxford glossary through...
Well, there are 26 letters in English... okay.
But I wonder of only one letter today...
My favorite letter for sure this is "C".
It should be pronounced like long sound to "see",
or maybe like "sea"?... I'm little confused...
Do I just dream "to see sea"?... What sound to choose?
There are lot of some words is beginning with "C"...
But this letter is tricky... Let's figure out... don't go to sea...
So, at the beginning of words our "C" reads like "K"...
I've not foreseen it in such summer day...
Let us check this... Let us to see...
Coffee, Courage, Control, Christmas and Color...
Cosset, Cake, Cognac and Curare?!... Caress...
Curiosity, Cat, Coruscate and Cute [dress:))]...
And only sometimes it's pronounced as real sound "si".
Gently, politely, so touched... You can see...
Cygnus, Civility, Cells and ...Celine....
[Slender] Cypress...Celadon, Cedar, Cerulean...
Cyclone...Certainty, Celebrate, Centerpiece...
Center, Cicero... Cyclopedia... Circumstances...
So, strange letter the "C" can be soft, can be strong...
It's very special, try not to be wrong.
So, it seems we have figured it out...
One more surprise!!! It's like an discovery night!
There is a crooked letter that sounds like "C"...
Sensitive, Special, Smart, Super star,
Sumptuous, Sunny, Sweet, Smiling...
Sparkle, Stupefying, Splendid and Stunning,
Strikingly, Soulfully, Singing, Strong, Song.
Don't make a mistake... Try not to be wrong...

Open book

My life is like an open book.
Page after page... You read all this...
My family, siblings, my friends and my kids...
Music, career, my visits and trips...
My happiness, sadness, my joy and my health...
My troubles, disquiets and worries...
My memories, fears and sorrows...
All like in the palm of your hands...
My fragile life as crystal-made....
I often want to hide a bit...
Transparent life... I wanna shade...
Be careful when flipping through my sheets.
They say if we usually open a book,
and the book opens us up.
Well, read, discuss, form own outlook...
Take my story and fill your life up...
I was born to sing songs for you.
And I hope this made someone feel better, grow up...
My songs have sometimes helped you...
You have found good friends... your life was light up.
Well. But leave me a few pages as well.
Only for me... Just a few sheets of my life.
Don't try to open what I don't want to tell...
This is my secret... My soul... My love...
Thank for your love and disregard of self.
You know that I sing for you all, touch your hearts.
You feel that with my voice I give you myself...
Piece after piece... my light, breath, soul parts.
Look through my life as opened book...
Turn over all my pages... one after one...
But please do not look only back...

Not so quickly, but I run...
Still waiting for a lot of things...
For everyone.. and just for me...
Be gentle when you touch my life.
Don't cut my wings. I'm alive.

Trace in your soul

No way to explain...
But you'll feel it again!
You will feel that your soul
Crazy strives for someone...
Your hot blood will wake up...
And you couldn't more wait...
No one second of time...
no one!... no one!...
No way to explain...
Were you getting afraid?...
Better stress less...
No love and caress?...
Do you know, that
Fortune likes brave...
Well... please be fearless,
To be happy, princess...
Say you need me... I miss you...
I am died almost...
I can't be "nobody" for you.
I can't dance with a ghost.
I do need to feel you.
Don't be silent, my dearest.
You have taken my heart,
I still love you... but I'm died almost...
I don't know for sure...
Are you reward or my curse?
Talk to me, my allure.
Don't be as an evil ghost!
Could you don't slip away...
Your hands and your voice...
Shoulders, eyes, and the smile...

I am crazy of you... and you know why.
No way to explain...
But you touched my soul...
I'm losing and losing control...
You prefer to be an inaccessible face...
This is a problem for me...
You may never see me in that case.
But, you'll never forget me!
I'll be always in your soul as trace...

Message to you

It's very hard to love you, honey.
Across the endless deepest ocean...
In front of millions of eyes...
I miss you much and show my devotion.
I want to touch, to shelter in your arms,
And not to move... to stay by you...
To dream together, warm you with my love...
To share my world with you... It's absolutely true...
I always have a talk with you...
And every day, and every night...
Why are you silent? ... So cold...
Amazing... Moon light Goddess... Why?
My lovely beauty, only one,
My Snow-Ice Princess,
Will I ever back my heart?
Or is it so hopeless?
There are some certain souls
"on one wave" in a space.
Like our stars in sky...
They wander millions of ways...
They're looking for each other, waiting for...
Sometimes it takes whole life... or more ...
They are so free like soaring birds.
They feel close soul light
and don't need any words!...
For sure, I could find you again,
in the next our cycles of life...
Is it not better to have a talking today?
Let's take a chance... let's take a chance...
Well, I'm a dreamer, romancer...
I came up it "all by myself"...

My brain is a prankster...
What should I do with my sense?
Do not hurt those who are in love with us...
They're already punished enough....
I am in love... It's not funny for me... no new.
It's a great privilege to be crazy of you...
Do you hear me, cute?
It is so hard... so hard...
Don't let me leave you...
I'm for laughing, not for crying by heart...

Don't wake me up

Don't wake me up, don't wake me up.
Do not return my madness... follies,
My crazy fleeting dreams and jollies,
Do not return! Don't wake me up!...
Don't tell me name, this memory is
The greatest torment of my soul,
Like a native song for an exile
Who finds far from his sweet home...
Don't resurrect, don't resurrect
Misfortunes that forgotten me,
Give rest to passion. I'm a stone.
Don't open wounds... leave me alone.
Don't wake me up, don't wake me up.
Do not return my madness, follies,
My crazy fleeting dreams and jollies,
Do not return! Don't wake me up!...
I tear off mask! I'm in front of you!
It's easier to feel a grief of self-will,
Than show you my false calmness,
Deceptive peace. I love you... still.

My autumn

In one spring day, in sunny city
I was born with lucky star.
Is that why I'm so pretty?
I have got the sun inside...
Many summers, springs and winters
have already flown away...
I remember something... someone...
with love and kind every day..
My "fall" is beautiful with many paints...
Cold angry rains sometimes...
then warm and sunny days...
You can see everything...
Sun... winds... and mists...
Gold, silver, emerald...
Red, green... Such endless list!
Blue, turquoise, orange, white...
I'm often wistful... dream of you...
I want to love ... To say you *"Je vous aime"*...
I wanna lose my sense of time with you,
My eyes sparkle with shine flame...
It's fire of my heart...
it doesn't want to go away!
I want to be loved by you,
I want to fly forgetting who I am....

Taking you away

May I take you away from loneliness?
Tell me something about yourself...
Do you have something new?
Your projects... boys... worries...
Why I don't see happy face?
Let me say something you.
I will take you away from the stupid fusses...
May I kiss you, my darling?
Tender touch to your lips?
Could you give me a kiss?
Everything else is scurry and bustle...
Only close relations...
Feel my loving heart beats...
What's that? Is your heart beating faster?
I don't want to let you out of my arms...
I'll take you away from the hustle and bustle,
Hug me... this game for adults
takes two persons, two charms...
I will steal you from troubles and sorrows...
May I pat you like a baby... on head?
Listen to me... everything passes....
And your troubles will pass too....
Only trust me... and let's go ahead!
I will shelter you from heartaches and wounds...
I'm near... Let's whisper with you...
You can tell me about
all your worries and moods...
I can feel your concerns cause I really love you.
With me, you can be whatever you want....
Dream, laugh, get angry, teach me how to do...
Do whatever you want, just don't be so cold!

I want to admire. I want to love you...
I'm crazy... it's a kind of madness!
I trust that my dreams will come true.
My life is rife with suddenness...
I'll do my best for you...
I don't need permission to love you...
Please read what was written above...
My precious, my sweetheart, my love!

Calling me

Why I am not a wind?
I would rush to you
sweeping all in my path...
I would like to be a sunbeam,
gently touch you and wake you up...
I would like to be a delicate water,
hold you sweetly and soft in my arms...
Do you think it's unwary and mindless?
Why, how and who sent me this love?
Cupid boy, are you blinded or cruel?
Is this your playing, farce or reward?
I feel my way takes me to you...
I'm courageous and strong.
Call me... and I will cross all the seas...
lakes, rivers and oceans... non-stops...
I will overcome forests, fields, hills,
the dried deserts and snow tops...
I remember you said that
you can't trust everyone....
It's right, darling.. great!
But I'm not everyone,
I am only one.
Just wait for me!
Only wait!

A few words to heaven

I wanna ask you to today....
Don't take away... don't take away!!!
Please leave me her... don't touch...
You've already taken so much.
I'm not asking you to give me anything.
Don't take my love from me!
Please... Only this one thing!
I know well we've came to leave.
But don't rush me.
I really love! Believe...
The whole world's nothing...
Don't give me anything,
just leave me love!
just leave me her...
Why do I need my life,
sunrises and sunsets?
Why do I need birdsongs?
I don't need beauty,
whole world wealth...
Don't take my love!
Light of my life...
Dream of my night...
I'm praying... crying...
ask you to...
Don't stop our flying!...
I wanna ask you to today....
Don't take away... don't take away!!!

If tomorrow I die...

Well... If tomorrow I die...
No matter where, no matter why...
I'll stop my way.. so sorrow...
what if I die tomorrow?!
They say that nothing changes,
all things are as before...
that is a little strange...
just no one to wait for...
The same the sun, and wind, and rains,
the same green trees, blue sky and seas...
White snow tops with gray-red rocks...
Whole our world as colored box...
And only you will not have me...
no one to wait for... no me...
I won't you hug, I won't you kiss ...
no whisper, voice and... will you miss?...
What am I here? Why? What for?!
I haven't been here before....
And won't be after... Who am I?
Am I just spirit in your mind?...
I'd like your heart will be my home
in whole our beautiful great world.
We have to fall to up and fly...
We need to lose before to find...
And should we cry
then laughing later?...
Is it so need to feel some pain
before to feel some pleasant matter?
I really have to die
to live in you forever... Why?

Are these your rules,
my harsh sweet life?
You know... I'm ready...
to do my best for you...
I am from new your angels...
I'm sent for loving you...

My heart is crying

Hush now, please… and look around …
The gentle sun and blue-blue sky...
Love is a gift... such kind of light!...
All lovers dream... they wanna fly...
they wanna smile, give love... all right!...
Then why are these so bitter tears?
Please, hush... My heart is crying... please...
Why do you so... so miss?
I don't grasp you... it's so stupid...
and someone else is getting fun...
Just have a look!... She doesn't need me!
I couldn't even light her up.
Forgive me please my poor heart!
You were so crazy... Stop! Give up!...
You don't believe, my broken heart...
She doesn't need me... time is up!
I don't want to... I don't want, but...
Love is destroying soul, breaking heart....
I don't want to... but I'm crying...
I don't want to... but I'm dying...
Because I love you... don't want to...
I feel... I'm burning... burning from inside...
Where is just single sign from you?...
Does love create...?! It's stupid lie!
There is no force that's more ruinous!
I am a lonely ghost of darkness night.
Wait for a little... and keep your silence...
More one black hole will born tonight...

Simple difficult questions

Please tell me why I'm doing this?
Why am I crazy... and I miss?
Why am I looking for your look,
My tender lovely "open book"?
Why am I waiting for your sign,
My fair lady, my sunshine?...
Why do I think about you
And whisper only "I love you"?...
I don't feel confidence, my sweet...
If our eyes can only meet...
I will not say you anything...
But you will hear my heartbeats...
I wanna drown in your eyes...
Where is my wariness and wise?
My pretty Angel, what to do?
I could do everything for you!

The blues...

All has been said... I don't tell anything...
Just take my hand. Give me a hug and
whisper to me something...
Your French is like a miracle
for treating of my heart...
I drink your words... drop after drop...
like magic and sweet drug...
or maybe wine?... don't know what...
I feel it's so fine!
One more your word... your whisper,
I feel your breath... and no red line ...
only your lips... your kisses... one more love sip...
What do you feel?.. Is it absurd?...
Maybe... But I'm fine...
Right now you are smiling me...
And nothing more is in this world.
Another breath... we're cheek to cheek...
This is as old as our world...
Let's dance.. This is the time for it...
Time for love dance...
I LOVE you... I love YOU...
Your voice sounds miracle inside me.
Just rhythm and blues...
Just blues and rhythm...
Give me a chance... Let's take a chance...
I don't see anything... just feel your flame...
and one more kiss... more hug... and rhythmic dance...
I love your French...
I'm suffocating... from crazy tenderness...
from your caress...

I'm drowning... deeper... deeper... down... no air...
your shoulders burn my palms like flame.
You are my breath. I'm calling you by name...
I'm flying by my own... I've absolutely lost my brain...
Oh, shit.... Alarm! Alarm!
It's time to wake me up!
I have to run for working...
and very quickly run!:))

It's cold...

It's very cold to me, because...
I've lost my heart... I am in love with ghost.
You are inside me... But I'm not with you...
You have to be! I wanna really love you.
I feel you well, though I can't touch...
I'm calling you... I want too much...
Just come to me... just hug and kiss!
You don't imagine how I miss!!!
It's cold... infinite days and long-long nights...
I'm very tired... Where's the light?
I'm waiting for... please come and warm...
It's cold to me... I am alone.
I don't want live without you...
Without you ... all things are wrong...

Thoughts under rain

It's raining... sky is crying rain...
That's angels are so sorry,
they have brought only pain...
They badly played the darts
and couldn't bridge two hearts...
I hear your heartbeat in the distance.
You easy entered my soul
Without any my assistance...
You are inside me, like my part.
You didn't feel any resistance...
You stole my heart
but something's wrong.
We're still apart...
you don't hear my song...
I love you so much...
I want to be with you...
I fall into the sky
when mentally touch you...
I know you can feel
my flame, which is inside,
through a great distance,
which separating us.
I'm not afraid of heights...
I'm not afraid of deepness...
I'm afraid to leave you.
I'm afraid of weakness.
I'm diving for you...
I'm sinking to the bottom...
There is no new life...
only ghosts dark begotten...
I am fighting for you

I am doing my best.
And what are you doing?... and you?!
You are silent... no warm or kindness.
I think it is easier to recover dead lands...
Such cruel days...
hearts-broken time!
I have to say it is not mine!
I want to fly, not crawl!
I want to love... feel soul...
I am delicate, fragile and so on...
but I am ready to fight for you… even alone.
You're talking to me with someone else's words...
you're talking to me with your songs quotes...
Please say something yourself.
Don't let me leave you... It's wrong...
Could you please talk to me
my lovely Headstrong!
I'm looking for you.
Tears are pouring down like rain...
I am loosing my brain...
I have already lost it...
I can feel only pain...

Too much?

"I feel that everything burned down.
I told you everything... that's all...
I'm not the one you think about...
and maybe not the one you want...
Forgive me for my crazy love...
You're too high... I'm on the ground...
I tried to touch you... gently touch...
You didn't feel... I have to leave you now...
You don't need love... You don't want touch...
Too much for me... It is too much..." –
What's that? ...It's speech of mind,
which talks to me all days and nights.
It is my clever brain... it hurts me so much...
Big thanks to you my pretty head,
you are so clever, very smart...
You wish me only good things... but...
YOU kill my heart!... you kill my HEART!
Stop, brain! Please... It's so hard...
let's listen whisper of my heart:
"I want to feel. I need to love...
hold me close to feel alive.
It's nothing bad...
I want to be with you.
I'm not a crazy, not a mad.
I'm like free wind... keep in your mind...
I'm warm and tender... joyful, kind...
I love you so much.
I wanna stand by you.
I will be gentle in my touch...
I want to be with only you..."
What can you say? Too much... too much...

Your kiss

I live and therefore I love ...
I love and feel I'm alive...
You know, honey, it's not easy ...
Without you I can't survive.
What my love is?
What is my love?
I want to kiss, I wanna touch...
I wanna carress you so much.
Let's talk with you...
Let's hug and kiss...
Without you..
it's like abyss...
It's all black–dark...
There is no bliss.
What is my life
without your kiss?

A call

My brown-eyed, my lovely queen...
I don't know why... I'm really keen...
I think... I'm wandering alone...
Nothing lasts forever... It's well known...
How can we love?... how to believe? ...
If you know that we've come to leave...
To love or not?... "...To be or not to be..."
I feel you have encourage me...
Your eyes are showing me the light...
Like nice bright stars in long black night.
What should I do? Where is my way?
Just look at me... don't look away...
"...*Encore un soir...*" What can I say concerning life?...
Love is in core! It makes us happy and alive...
You are my air, my respiration,
You are the source of inspiration.
It doesn't matter how long...
It doesn't matter right or wrong!...
I love you... and...
If you need me...
Just take my hand...
Just let it be...

The first winter day

It's night, snowflakes are spinning quietly...
and glittering in the moonlight...
White winter days are starting lightly,
and Christmas will be soon... delight ...
I love this white calm time...
Another year has passed...
It's time to think of future,
remember our past...
I can't forget you, lovely...
I'm like a wounded bird.
I cannot fly; I'm lonely,
I cannot sing my song...
It's like I'm in cage...
I deeply hide my heart.
it's frozen for an age.
My fire is deep inside;
While, I have kept all colors...
All colors of my love...
But... where are you, my darling?
I want to be alive...
I want to breathe together,
to have one sky for two,
to be with you in any weather...
drink sweet hot chocolate,
to dream and talk to you.
I need your warmth and your affection.
I want to feel your gentle touch.
I know what I'll wish this Christmas...
It will be really not too much:)...
I want to love... I wish to kiss...
I want to smile with happiness...
I want to touch... don't want to miss,
I want to feel your joyfulness!

Dark black and white

Cold winter night...
Dark black and white...
I cannot sleep;
Endless white light...
Prickly snowflakes,
frosty white plaid...
it covers trees, lake...
I feel so bad...
Black hides in white...
the fire goes out...
I lost you tonight.
You didn't find out...
Such a dark night!...
Dark black and white...
White snowflakes;
I caught you... almost...
It was my mistake!
my beautiful ghost.
Don't play with my love.
It's a very hot flame...
I'm burning inside;
Please, darling, don't play.

Christmas wishes

I'm far away...
Beyond deep blue ocean.
I can fondle you just with words...
and send you love, my good mood and emotions.
It's like I touch you, kiss and embrace.
Open your heart for my tenderness.
It's winter now. Christmas' coming soon.
It's a great time. It's wonderful.
I wish you a Merry Christmas!!!
I wish you love and happiness...
I wish you to get well soon,
forget about sadness!
I will come to you and ask how you are...
I will hug you tight and ask to *"regardez-moi"*
You will answer, "Okay... I've been waiting for you..."
And we'll run away... I'll be crazy of you.
I'll whisper to you... I'll hug you tight;
I will kiss your smile... if you don't mind.
To see rainbow... we have to stand heavy rain...
I will stand by you... We will win your pain.
Green-blue spring will come after cold-white time.
It's all planet rules, it's not only mine.
After dark black night, the sun ups again.
All bad things will pass... You'll forget your pain!

My prayer

Lord! Give me wings...
to fly across the ocean.
And give me strength
to save my Love.
I don't have other needs...
no more emotions...
I want to stand by you...
as angel, like your guard.
I will disperse all clouds,
all troubles and all ailments,
I'll even find good knight
on miracle white horse.
Becoming hiding ghost,
I'll make a fairy tale for you...
I'll break my heart
to give you tender words.
From broken pieces of my mind,
I'll make few stars to your blue sky ...
I will become as spring warm wind
Just talk to me sometimes...
I'll take away from you
all illness and disease,
all grief and sadness...
Let me do this... please!

White

You know why I don't like quiet winter;
These mono-color pics of snow... blue-blue skies...
It's like results of work of black-white printer!
I'm going crazy from this silence and cold shine!...
I don't like white... It's color of all sorrows... sadness...
While it is true, it's color of the light...
Life's hidden under snow sparkling blanket...
White frost... ice emptiness... I don't like White...
You know, White assimilates
the other colors of the light,
as longing can absorb all feelings,
fun, all joyfulness and love...
And only pure crystal can help to find
all hidden colors from inside.
My soul sings about love,
My heart is bursting from my chest...
and tears.... and joy.... and happiness...
Don't rush to tell me "no"... Don't rush...
And don't believe that time has passed...
It's time for us ... it's time for us.
I'm like a flame. I love a spring.
My favorites are Red and Green.
I love a life, You are my light.
Let's think to get all colors from your White.

Feelings and wishing

Why do we need some words?
They just confuse our souls...
I definitely feel something...
I feel that something wrong...
Why do you need this? To look strong?...
I see your eyes... They are so crying...
They burn like wildfire... I feel it!
Why are your lips still so silent?...
It's violent... Is what you need?
I'm meant for love. I'm not from iron...
I've given up without war...
Sometimes it's better to be happy...
not fight and win for looking strong.
I wish you a Merry Christmas!
I wish you a happy year.
May everyone be healthy...
I pray... may all wars end...
We all were born for loving,
for giving happiness.
May you forget all fighting...
Light up... and God you bless!

Calling you

Lonely cold... and lonely dark...
There is no a single spark...
Lonely you and me tonight.
No light... cold wind and night...
There is no way... I'm trapped..
All by myself... I am as mad...
No advice...I'm waiting for...
I can not take it anymore!...
I want your voice... I want your touch...
my heart is beating so much...
I dream of you... It's so cool...
be sure, I know that I'm fool...
I have to get away from you...
But I'm too weak...cause I love you...
I'm calling you... I'm on your way...
Just hear my call... Just feel my pray...

The reason for to be

The basis... the reason of all...
What is in basis of life?...
What always inflames our soul?...
Love is the source of my fire...
I am the flame... I am the light!
I can you warm... be your delight...
to give you joy in day and night...
Stop!... Hush!...
It seems that something is not right...
Don't rush...
I ask to you... don't rush...
I come to you with open heart;
with pure soul, with open arms...
Please, take my warmth, don't be apart...
I'm so crazy of your charms.
But give me back a bit... I miss...
I have to feel your fire... please...
I don't know why... why do you need me? ...
Maybe to hug... perhaps, to kiss...
to talk?... to smile... caress, dream, miss?
Take off your battle armor... please...
Don't think about it...
Just feel my gentle touch....
I hug you... hear your heartbeat;
I want to kiss... Is not too much?
I will be there...
I fell in love... I feel like I broke free...
I will be there...
I feel you are my reason for to be...

What to do?

I ran away again...
It seems I am afraid of you.
I am exhausted by this pain...
I'll never say that I love you...
Please keep your soul safe,
don't ask to be with you.
You have to go own way,
don't dream that I'll kiss you...
Why are you still here?
I am not for you, honey.
Please don't eyes on me...
I'm not ice to melt in the sun...
How did you get inside me?
I don't want to think of you...
Why do you need me? Tell me!
I don't want... but I love you...
I really want to say adieu...
It would be better for me and you…
But what to do with our hearts?
They will never be renewed...

Enough...

Enough... I can't drink more...
there is no wine in bar...
I am alone without you...
How could you say "goodbye"?
My heart is so crying...
My lips remember you...
I can't forget your heat;
Impossible... I deeply love you...
I hate!... I'm calling you!!!
Take your mobile!.. just take!
Who is... who is with you?
I'm crazy... white turned dark black...
I can not live without you!!!
I want to feel your touch!
Say me "hello" again... I'll kiss you...
I miss you so much...
Enough... I feel I'm dying...
My sky is dark... black sun!
I close my eyes... I'm flying...
You were so wrong... my one...

Corrida

I've been waiting for you for so long.
It's time! I'm here...
I'm standing in front...
I am handsome and strong.
You came out to win.
It's your rules... It's your dream...
You are ready to kill...
Why do you like such a brutal extreme?...
You are confident that...
I was born to be dead!
Take a look... there are thousands eyes...
they look forward to us...
They need show... need blood...
No passion in life?... no light?
Well, let's start our battle!
Even if I don't want any fight...
You have trained very well...
Just don't look into eyes...
Our world is so cruel...
We play different roles in a life...
doesn't matter the price...
even if it is LIFE...
Are you ready to strike?
Do what you have to do...
Take a knife... Take your knife...
Pierce my heart... don't think of...
I don't want to live anymore...
My life is void of...
I didn't know love...
But I was dreaming to fly...

Espada, be strong!...
Well, it's done, matador.
Now I'm ready to die...
Such a pain!...
Such blue sky...

Wild love

I'm tired be alone,
it's very hard for heart...
I don't want being stone.
My life is not chessmat!...
I am in love with Queen...
and I could play this game...
but would prefer some real...
I want to touch... okay?
I'm calling you... and ask to run away...
Life is much better than chess play.
It's not just squares – black and white...
In real life we may decide...
You are my love, you are my dream...
Wind brings me name... Celine... Celine...
I lose myself when think of you...
I don't need life without you...
I kiss your cheek... I take your palm...
I'm begging you: "please stay, don't run"
Where is my friend, my lovely wind?...
Whisper again... Celine... Celine...
I'm not afraid to say to you
that I love you... I dream of you...
My love is wild... it is like flame...
My soul is pure... please don't me blame...

Hello

Hello... how are you?
I'm sorry,
I shouldn't be so far...
You know well
I love you...
I left with you my heart.
I've almost dead
without you...
Please kiss me
like you can...
I cannot breathe
cause missed you...
I'm sorry...
I'm like a mad...
I don't want live
without your eyes...
I hear your voice at night...
May I embrace you?
I feel touch...
Your heart beats
so much...
Don't say again
that we should not...
you shouldn't tell me lies...
I see your eyes...
I feel that souls
decided all for us.

Windy mood

Today my mood is like the wind...
I want to talk... and maybe dream...
About what? what do you think?
Why is the sky blue... why is grass green?
why is the night dark?... sunrise is pink...
why have we met? What does it mean?
...Why do you smile?... So many "why"?...
I'm getting crazy from your smile...
I wanna kiss... Don't ask me "why"?...
My mind is empty from your smile...
Okay... I'm ready... try again...
So, what do you think?...
No... no... please wait...
What do you feel? –
This is the main!...
When sun is shining brightly...
when sky is blue... and grass is green...
when I kiss you... what do you feel?
I feel so good... I see your smile...
Don't ask me "why"... Don't ask me "why"...
I'm getting crazy from your smile...
just wanna kiss... you know "why"...

My soul speaks to yours

I am from sunny city.
That's why my heart is hot...
I know what is desert...
That's why I'm so strong.
I know price for friendship,
I know real love...
I like snow tops, ice water,
hot sand and blue-blue sky...
They say, "it doesn't happen...
Life is not a fairytale..."
and "only fool can rush in"...
I do all what I may...
I'm learning to love you...
to love you on a distance....
with nothing in return...
It is not easy... mistress...
What can I do for you?
Please, tell me what to do...
I learn to love you...
I learn to be without you...
I learn to breathe alone...
I'm learning not to wait for you...
I'm trying to be strong...
it's awful if I'm used...
There is no one around...
Guitar sounds soft...
It's so touched... I'm crying
because this gentle song...
I dream of you... I'm silent...
My body's dancing slowly,
I feel my sense is flying...

My soul speaks to yours...
I've found you... just trust me...
I am surprised like you...
but anyway... let's fly with me...
I need to be next you.

You didn't say hello to me...

You didn't say hello to me...
it doesn't matter...
with someone... and somewhere...
sometimes it happens...
It's time to say goodbye...
What stupid words!...
you didn't hear whisper and my cry...
Love hurts!...
It's all in vain...
Clouds should meet clouds in the sky...
it's known well...
But!...
How did you rush into my heart?.
I am like fool from Elvis song!...
You are my blessing... and...
your voice... your eyes... your smile...
I rushed towards...
I have to stop...
I had to say goodbye... not sing love song by words...
Why do I need this crazy music in my soul?
What do I need at all?
It's just a dreams!...
All say, "Come on! Drop fantasies and nonsense!
why do you need extreme?"
You know what... I have been changed...
I'll never be the same...
I want to live...
I want to be a flame...
Okay... I see I broke the rules again...
I talk about love instead of "farewell pain".

Where can I get a force?
Please, God! I am in love...
Give me some patience and wisdom...
to wait for... to believe... to love...

My dream

The night is outside...
Let's leave all troubles there...
I want to ask you to...
No...no... forget... don't care...
Don't talk... let's all be quiet
about something own,
about yours and mine...
How quickly time goes on...
Few seconds... years... it's time!...
Something was lost already...
Something can still be find...
Let's talk with you... I'm ready...
How quickly time goes on!...
You know well I love you...
I'm flying in this flow...
I see... I feel... and I can do...
what never did before.
My soul sings only for you...
I wasn't waiting for...
I see you smile me...
and I can do it all!...
I am a crazy dreamer...
My heart will go on!...
Let's dream and fly with me...
I'm flying on my own...
Be own life's designer...
I'm waiting for... come on!
I come to you with open arms...
Last winter gave me you...
You quickly captured my soul
to land of dreams with you...

I'm flying now in this flow...
I see... I feel... I do...
like never... never did before...
I wanna be with you.

What is Love

So many people with whom you can go to bed...
and only a few with whom you want
to wake up in the morning...
and parting each time to look back,
to smile... to wait for... to worry.
So few people with whom you could dream...
look like a child at a red fire or clouds...
together enjoy vanilla ice cream,
write cute words in the sand for our lovers...
So many people to simply live with...
to drink coffee or tea, to think of...
with whom you can do something...
enjoy... not to love... to be close...
So few with whom you can be silent,
Who understand your look and half of any word...
for whom you take a pain or any violence...
you take it all as a reward.
That's how we freeze our hearts...
We meet so easily... parting painless...
Because there are so many... with whom we want to part...
and only a few with whom we want to wake up every day.
We are in a hurry... work, life, our business...
Who wants to hear something has to stop...
You know... on the run you notice just appearance...
Just stop a little... if you want to feel my soul.
We choose with our heart according to our mind...
Sometimes we are afraid... and don't respond to a smile,
We open our soul only to...
to one with whom we want to wake up every time.
How few of them, with whom we can feel some things.
With whom we share sorrow, joy and love...
perhaps because of them we get our wings ...
We fall in love and crazy love this life.

Smile

Smile, my honey.
I'm missing your smiles.
I want to see shining
of your beautiful eyes...
I feel your wild tenderness.
I'm melting... I burn...
Please back to your passion,
for that you were born!...
Someone may be calm...
but it's not really me!...
How beautiful you are!
I'm in love so deeply...
I whisper to you... and I cry!
let's remember with you
how to fly!
Please, don't kidding with me,
don't pretend...
Share your worries and joy ...
don't be sad.
I am here... please look at me
and let's start...
I will always love you...
even burning my heart.

Printed in the United States
by Baker & Taylor Publisher Services